The
of Loony Driving Laws

The Little Book of Loony Driving Laws

Christine Green

Illustrated by

Besley

www.vitalspark.co.uk

The Vital Spark is an imprint of
Neil Wilson Publishing Ltd
303 The Pentagon Centre
36 Washington Street
GLASGOW
G3 8AZ

Tel: 0141-221-1117
Fax: 0141-221-5363
E-mail: info@nwp.co.uk
http://www.nwp.co.uk

ISBN 1-903238-83-8

Typeset in Bodoni
Designed by Mark Blackadder

Printed and bound by Oriental Press, Dubai

Contents

Introduction

Long gone are those relaxing days when driving was more of a pleasure than a never-ending procession of exasperated motorists each vying for their own space, dodging in and out of the traffic like Jack Russell terriers on heat. Nowadays it is everyone for themselves ... road rage is on the increase, road etiquette is a thing of the past and you daren't even glance at a fellow motorist in case you are misunderstood. And, of course, driving is about as regulated a private undertaking as you can get. To drive we need to have a licence, to have a licence we have to pass a test; we need to understand road usage laws and our cars have to be insured as well as roadworthy and so it goes on ...

Bring back the horse and carriage – life was easier then, there was less hassle, less bad temper and fewer road users. But even in those simple days we realised that we had to regulate the movement of traffic. So laws were passed wherever there was horse-drawn traffic and these were altered when motor vehicles were invented. Cars have changed

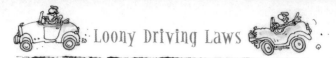

over the past century, but some of the people who
created the laws governing driving seem not to have.
Driving laws the world over are frequently quite
loony as you are about to find out.

Christine Green, 2005

IN AUSTRALIA ...

... all taxicabs are supposed carry a bale of hay in their trunk. This law was created when horse-drawn cabs were in use.

... it is a crime in some states to leave your car keys in an unattended vehicle.

... according to the Offence Act 1966 an edict was passed in the city of Melbourne banning anyone from driving a goat or dog which was attached or harnessed to a vehicle in a public place.

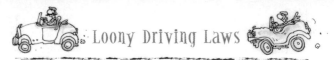

... one law in the Australian legal archives states that cars parked in public places must be locked but the windows must be opened to no more than the width of a hand.

IN BELGIUM ...

... the law decrees that a driver who needs to turn through oncoming traffic has the right of way unless he slows down or stops.

IN BERMUDA ...

... it is illegal to drive at over 20mph.

... tourists are banned from hiring cars and may only travel by moped, bus or taxi.

... each household can only have one car.

... cars cannot be more than 67 inches (1.7 m) wide or 169 inches (4.3m) long.

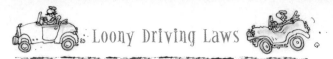

IN BULGARIA ...

... women drivers can be fined up to £200 if they are caught wearing shoes with four-inch heels.

... when vehicles are entering the country the tyres on every vehicle have to be disinfected.

IN CAMBODIA ...

... right-hand-drive vehicles are banned in order to control the smuggling of cars from Thailand. Furthermore all legal RHD vehicles have to be converted to left hand drive at the owner's expense.

IN CANADA ...

... working on one's car in public in Kanata, Ontario is prohibited.

... motorists living in Montreal may not wash their car in the street, nor may they park their car in such a way that is obstructing their own drive.

... in parts of Canada you are not allowed to fix 'for sale' signs on the windows of your vehicle.

... car owners who live in the provinces of Quebec and Newfoundland are not allowed to have personalised license plates.

... in Ontario a vehicle displaying a 'slow vehicle' sign but found to be motoring at 'normal speeds' will be stopped and the driver fined.

... although the speed limit in Ontario is 80kph for motorcars, cyclists have the right of way.

... a $5 fine will be given to anyone riding in a horse-drawn open sleigh on Ontario's roads if the horse does not have two bells, either attached to the harness, or the sleigh.

... any pet found roaming freely within 30 metres (100 feet) of the centre of the highway will incur the pet's owner a fine of $100. Should the event happen a total of three times in one year then the fine rises to $500.

... after the 1st December 1922 there was a problem for automobile drivers crossing the border between New Brunswick and Nova Scotia. New Brunswick switched to driving on the right-hand side of the road on that date but Nova Scotia stayed on the left-hand side. Drivers crossing the border in both directions had to change to the other side of the road immediately. It took four and a half months to sort out!

IN CHINA ...

... jaywalking is banned. If a jaywalker is hit by a car, it's the pedestrian's fault.

... according to Article 40 of the Beijing Traffic Laws, drivers of motor vehicles who stop at pedestrian crossings are likely to receive a warning or a fine.

....as a way of controlling noise in the coastal city of Yantai lawmakers banned drivers from sounding their car horns in urban districts. Furthermore no sirens are allowed.

... the first known regulation of road etiquette dates to 1100BC. The *Book of Rites* stated: 'The right side of the road is for men, the left side for women and the centre for carriages.' This rule applied only to the Zhou dynasty's wide official roads and was more concerned with protocol than avoiding head-on collisions.

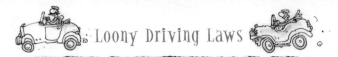

IN CYPRUS ...

... should you be driving anywhere near a hospital between the hours of 10pm – 6am the sounding of one's horn is strictly banned.

IN DENMARK ...

... legislation used to require that a full vehicle inspection was carried out prior to setting off. This included checking underneath the vehicle for hidden children.

... technically all automobiles should still be preceded by a man on foot warning horse-drawn carriages of any imminent danger.

CRUNCH   SCREECH

IN FINLAND ...

... the Helsinki Police do not issue parking tickets to motorists who illegally park, but instead deflate their car tyres.

... speeding fines are linked to income, so the richer you are, the more you pay. Anssi Vanjoki, 44, a director of Nokia, was ordered to pay a fine of 116,000 Euros in 2002 after being caught speeding in Helsinki.

IN FRANCE ...

... before the French revolution the aristocracy travelled quickly on the left-hand side and forced the peasantry over to the right. After the revolution aristocrats joined the peasants on the right-hand side. A keep right rule was then introduced in Paris in 1794 and later Napoleon enforced this rule in all countries occupied by his armies. This is how the Swiss, Germans, Italians, Poles and Spanish all came to drive on the right.

IN GERMANY ...

... good driving etiquette is vital when driving on the roads in Germany; bad manners could result in having to pay a hefty fine especially if you make a rude hand gesture to a fellow motorist or insult a police officer.

IN GIBRALTAR ...

... to reduce excess noise within the town limits, motorists are banned from sounding their horns.

IN GREAT BRITAIN ...

... it was once mandatory that all London Hackney taxis had to carry a bale of hay and a sack of oats in their trunk in case they should come across a roaming horse.

... in London it is illegal to drive a car without sitting in the front seat.

... in theory *'if a self-propelled carriage is driven on the Queen's highway then a man must walk four miles in front waving a red flag by day and a red lantern by night'*.

… legislation was passed making it legal for a male to urinate in public, provided it was done so on the rear wheel of his motor vehicle with his right hand resting on his vehicle!

… It is illegal to drive a self-propelled carriage any faster than 4mph on the Queen's highway.

… in Savoy Court, the London street running from the Strand to the Savoy Hotel, cars must drive on the right.

… in Swindon it is possible to be fined up to £1,000 if found driving a vehicle with dirty number plates.

… taxi drivers are quite within their rights to ignore any potential customers who simply shout them down.

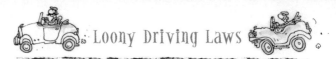

... taxi drivers are within their rights to decline a hire if the customer is suffering from cholera or the plague.

IN GREECE ...

... a driver's licence can be revoked if he is deemed poorly dressed or even appears to be unwashed.

... the number plates of illegally parked cars can be confiscated.

IN INDONESIA ...

... in East Timorese near to the city of Dili there appear to be no motoring regulations whatsoever. You have been warned!

IN ITALY ...

... having sex in the backseat of your car can land you in jail for up to three years. However, offenders can evade a prison sentence if the car's windows are covered to prevent passers-by from seeing inside.

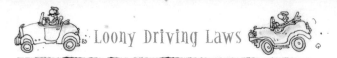

Loony Driving Laws

IN JAMAICA ...

... if a motorist is involved in an accident with a stray animal wandering into the road then the maximum that the animal's owner can be pursued for is $250.

IN JAPAN ...

... there are several driving offences. Pedestrians always have the right of way and drivers cannot turn at a junction on a red light as is allowed in the USA.

IN LUXEMBOURG ...

... although abolished in 2000, motorists once had to sound their horn when overtaking.

... when overtaking at night it is compulsory to flash the car's headlights.

... windshield wipers are compulsory ... but windshields are not!

24

Loony Driving Laws

IN MEXICO ...

… safety bicycles, boneshakers and other similar machines are banned from the centre of Mexico City.

… according to the law, bicycle riders may not lift either foot from the pedals in case they lose control.

… it is an offence to whistle, annoy or distract a cyclist.

… no horses or wheeled transport are allowed in Mexico City during Holy Week.

IN NIGERIA ...

… motorcycle taxi riders in northern Nigeria are banned from carrying Muslim female passengers. A public lashing is the penalty for ignoring the law.

… intolerant motorists in Lagos who drive on the wrong side of the road or jump curbs can be arrested, their vehicles impounded and have fines imposed of 25,000 naira ($200) along with mandatory psychiatric tests.

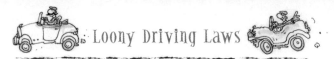

Loony Driving Laws

IN NEW ZEALAND ...

... drivers are on the left-hand side of the road but must give way to all traffic crossing or approaching from the right.

IN RUSSIA ...

... it is illegal to drive a dirty car.

Same here - 12 years for a nasty smear on the rear bumper-

Loony Driving Laws

IN SAN SALVADOR ...

... drunk drivers can be punished by death before a firing squad.

IN SAUDI ARABIA ...

... women are not allowed to drive cars.

... should an infidel accompany a Muslim then both are required to use the highways for infidels.

... on the spot driving fines can be as much as 900 Riyals (190 Euros)

... a standard parking fine is 500 Riyals (105 Euros) together with three days in prison.

... if you brake and do a U-turn in a car park the penalty is 500 Riyals and two days in jail.

... if you jump a red light the fine is 900 Riyals and three days in prison.

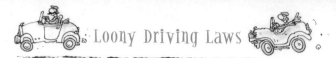

... motorists who display reckless driving and skidding are fined 1500 Riyals (316 Euros) with 20 days in prison and 20 lashes. If you happen to be a passenger in a recklessly driven car you will also be fined 1500 Riyals and receive 20 lashes ... but you won't go to jail!

IN SINGAPORE ...

... it is illegal to come within 50 metres of a pedestrian crossing the street.

IN SOUTH KOREA ...

... traffic police are legally obliged to report all bribes offered by motorists.

IN SWEDEN ...

... in 1965 motorists changed over to driving on the left-hand side of the road. This was carried out on a weekday at precisely 5.00pm in order to prevent people from waking up in the morning and forgetting which side of the road they should be on.

IN SWITZERLAND ...

… the Sabbath is vigorously upheld, and on Sundays people may not wash their cars.

… it is illegal to leave your keys inside an unlocked vehicle.

… it was once illegal to slam your car door shut.

IN THAILAND ...

… when a man is driving he must always wear a shirt.

... the larger the vehicle in Thailand the more it has 'right of way'. In other words buses and trucks take precedence over cars, cars take precedence over motorbikes and that leaves the poor cyclist at the end of the queue.

IN TURKEY ...

... a new Turkish directive requires motorists to carry at all times not only a red warning triangle but also a hygienic body bag suitable for transporting a corpse weighing up to 18st 12lb. Drivers have a limited time of three months to equip themselves with this or face a fine and up to six months in jail.

IN THE USA ...

... the personalised license plate 3M TA3 was banned after six months because when viewed in the rear-view mirror it said 'EAT ME'.

... the Code of Federal Regulations declares it illegal for US citizens to have any contact with extra-terrestrials or their vehicles.

Loony Driving Laws

IN ALABAMA ...

... drivers are not allowed to drive blindfolded.

... provided you have a lantern firmly attached to the front of your vehicle then it is perfectly legal to drive down a one-way street.

... the law states that it is a crime to keep more than 12 inoperable vehicles at the front of a house.

... it is illegal to drive barefoot.

... in the township of Downey washing one's car in the street is illegal.

... in the township of Alhambra it is illegal to park your car in the street overnight without a permit.

IN ARIZONA ...

... it is illegal to drive your car in reverse in Glendale.

... Arizona law states that any reflectors or lights mounted on to the front or front side of a car

should be of an amber colour. Any reflectors or lights on the back or side back of the car must be of a red colour; except for signal lights which can be red, yellow or amber and the light which illuminates the license plate must be white.

IN ARKANSAS ...

... after 9.00pm it is illegal for a person to sound the horn on a vehicle in any location where sandwiches or cold drinks are served.

... it is an offence to molest an automobile in Clinton.

IN CALIFORNIA ...

... elephants in San Francisco are banned from being walked down Market Street unless they are on a leash.

... you can be arrested for shooting animals from a moving vehicle unless that animal is a whale.

... in Santa Clara, San Francisco, bicycles may not be ridden without 'appropriate fashion accessories' anywhere in the county.

... it is illegal to wipe one's car with items of used underwear in San Francisco.

... unless being preceeded by a man carrying a lantern, motor vehicles are banned from being driven in the streets of Redlands.

... women cannot drive cars while dressed in a housecoat.

... a law states that: *No vehicle without a driver may exceed 60 miles per hour*.

... in Long Beach it used to be law that garages could only be used for car storage.

... in Los Angeles County an old law states that: *'Speed upon county roads will be limited to 10 miles an hour unless the motorist sees a bailiff who does not appear to have had a drink in 30 days, then the driver will be permitted to make what he can.'* Furthermore *'whoever operates an automobile on any public way – laid out under the authority of law recklessly or while under the influence of liquor shall be punished; thereby imposing upon the motorist the duty of finding out at his peril whether certain highways had been laid out recklessly or while under the influence of liquor before driving his car over them.'* Well, that's all clear then.

… drivers in Hemet should be aware that the driver of *'any vehicle involved in an accident resulting in death … shall immediately stop … and give his name and address to the person struck.'*

… the law bans anyone from washing their car in the street in the township of Downey.

… in Cathedral City it is illegal to sleep in a parked car.

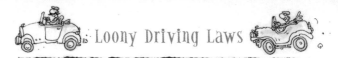

… in Hermosa Beach it is illegal to pour salt on the roads.

… in-car audio systems in Norco must not be audible from outside the car.

… the number of cars allowed on Catalina Island is strictly limited. The actual waiting time to get a permit for a car is 8-10 years. The result is that most residents drive gasoline-powered golf carts around the island.

… in certain areas of California motorcyclists are permitted to take part, and do so, in lane splitting. The literature accompanying the statute says that officers will try issuing the motorcyclist with a ticket, but only if the 'guilty party' seems affluent enough to afford it.

… technically riders of Harley-Davidsons are allowed to ride in a reclined position with feet up on the handlebars.

... a law from Wittier states that: *'Two vehicles which are passing each other in opposite directions shall have the right of way'*

IN COLORADO ...

... it used to be illegal to drive a black automobile on a Sunday in Denver.

... car dealers may not display their cars on a Sunday.

... all cyclists in Pueblo must carry gongs.

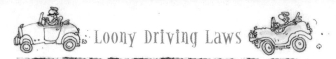
IN CONNECTICUT ...

... cab drivers caught carrying corpses in the township of Hartford may be liable to a $5 fine.

... in New Britain it is illegal for fire trucks to exceed 25 mph even when attending a fire.

... if you park more than 12 inches from the curb in New Britain you are liable to a $5 fine.

IN DELAWARE ...

... in the City of Fenwick Island legislation was passed whereby it was deemed unlawful for any

person to live, dwell, cook, sleep, change clothes
or use toilet facilities inside any vehicle within the
corporate limits of the Town of Fenwick Island.

… there is no legal requirement to wear a seat
belt.

… it is illegal to have a picnic on a highway in the
town of Fenwick Island.

IN FLORIDA ...

... if you hit a pedestrian in Sarasota you are fined $78.

... keeping a disused car on your property in Daytona is prohibited.

... a $50 fine will be levied in Cape Coral City on residents who sit on a sofa in their carports.

... if you park an elephant at a parking meter you must pay the fee just as though it were a vehicle.

... towing a sled behind one's bicycle in **Palm Bay** is banned.

... a judge in Florida has invented a rather creative way to punish DUI offenders by forcing them to put bumper stickers on their vehicles that reads, 'How's my driving? The judge wants to know.' There is a toll-free telephone number for motorists to call.

IN GEORGIA ...

... members of the state assembly cannot be ticketed for speeding while the state assembly is in session.

... state law prohibits people spitting from a car or bus, although spitting from a truck is OK.

IN IDAHO ...

... in the town of **Idaho Falls** anyone aged over 88 is forbidden to ride a motorcycle.

... in the township of **Montana** vehicles may not be operated with ice picks attached to the wheels.

... any police officer in Coeur d'Alene who suspects that sex is taking place in a vehicle must drive up from behind, honk his horn three times, and then wait two minutes before getting out of his vehicle to investigate.

... the following edict exists in the city of Pocatello: *'It is prohibited for pedestrians and motorists to display frowns, grimaces, scowls, threatening and glowering looks, gloomy and depressed facial appearances, generally all of which reflect unfavourably upon the city's reputation.'*

IN ILLINOIS ...

... no cars may be driven through the township of Crete.

... motorists are banned from driving in the left-hand-side lane of an interstate highway for more than one half miles. Anyone who does so and is caught can be fined $79.

... an automobile cannot impersonate a wolf in the township of Macomb.

… it is illegal in Evanston to change clothes in an automobile with the curtains drawn except in the case of fire.

… it is legally stipulated that a car must be driven with the steering wheel.

IN INDIANA ...

... backing a car into a parking space is illegal. An edict was passed banning drivers from backing into a car parking space because *it prevented the police from seeing your licence plate if needed.*

... motorists are prohibited to drive on Main Street in Evansville with their lights on.

IN IOWA ...

... it is unlawful to discriminate against a lawyer who is unable to drive a car.

IN KANSAS ...

... in Derby: *'It is unlawful for any person/s while operating a motor vehicle on the streets or highways of the city to accelerate or speed the vehicle in such a manner or to turn a corner in such a manner as to cause the tires to screech. Any person who violates any provision of this section is guilty of a misdemeanour and shall upon conviction be punished by a fine not to exceed $5,000, imprisonment for a period not to exceed thirty days or by both such fine and imprisonment.'*

… state law requires pedestrians on the highways at night to wear tail lights.

… in Wichita, before proceeding through the intersection of Douglas and Broadway, motorists are required to get out of their vehicle and fire.

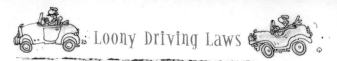
... in Russell, it is against the law to have a musical car horn.

... no motorist is allowed to leave his or her vehicle running unattended in the township of Salina.

... all cars entering the city limits of Lawrence are supposed to sound their horns to warn horses of their arrival.

IN KENTUCKY ...

... *'No female shall appear in a bathing suit on any highway within this state unless she is*

escorted by at least two officers or unless she be armed with a club. The provisions of this statute shall not apply to any female weighing less than 60 nor exceeding 200 pounds, nor shall it apply to female horses.

... dogs are banned from molesting cars in Fort Thomas.

IN LOUISIANA ...

... it is illegal for a woman to drive a car in New Orleans unless her husband is waving a flag in front of it.

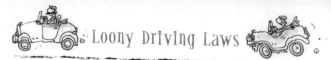
... by law fire trucks have to stop at all red lights in New Orleans.

IN MAINE ...

... it is illegal for a police officer to tell a person to have a nice day after pulling them over for a driving violation and issuing them with a ticket.

... cab drivers in the city of Buckfield are not allowed to charge a fare to any passenger who gives them sexual favours in return for a ride home from a nightclub or other establishment which serves alcoholic beverages.

IN MASSACHUSETTS ...

... state law bans pet gorillas from travelling in the back seat of a car.

... peeping into the windows of automobiles is forbidden in the township of Milford.

... passionate cab drivers are prohibited from making love in the front seat of their taxi during their shift.

... shaving while driving is banned.

... it is against the law to ride on the roof of your automobile in Springfield.

... it is against the law to attach a horse to a parking meter when the President is giving a speech on national television.

IN MIAMI ...

... 'no person shall operate a bicycle unless it is equipped with a bell or similar device capable of giving a signal loud enough to cover a distance of at least 100 feet, but no bicycle shall be equipped with, nor shall any person use upon a bicycle any siren or whistle'.

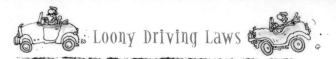
IN MICHIGAN ...

… couples are banned from making love in an automobile unless the act takes place while the vehicle is parked on the couple's own property.

… it is illegal to 'ogle' a woman from a moving car in Detroit.

… milkmen in Lower Bridge County are prohibited from riding on a bicycle whilst on duty.

… the speed limit in Port Huron for ambulances is 20mph.

IN MILWAUKEE ...

... you are not allowed to drive a car in the township of Cleveland whilst sitting on someone's lap.

... an old ordinance forbids parking for over two hours unless a horse is tied to the car.

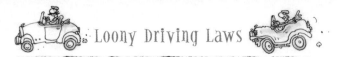

Loony Driving Laws

IN MINNESOTA ...

... driving a truck with dirty tyres is regarded as a public nuisance in the township of Minnetonka.

... all men driving motorcycles must wear shirts.

... no-one is allowed to sell a car on the Sabbath otherwise they risk spending one month in prison.

... motorists who are caught double parking can be put on a chain gang.

... driving laws state that: ' ... *all persons in the front seat of a car and all persons under 13 in the back seat must wear seatbelts. But if you are over 13 and in the back seat, the government has decided that, while you are still at risk, you are under considerably less risk than being in the front seat and if you are over 13 you can make your own decision about the seatbelt without worrying about facing any legal problems with it.*'

IN MISSISSIPPI ...

... it is illegal to drive around the square in the township of Oxford more than 100 times in a single session.

... motor vehicles are prohibited from the square in the township of Oxford.

... no horn honking is allowed for fear of startling horses in the township of Oxford.

... an old law states that if you are riding in a vehicle with a member of the opposite sex and you both have bare feet, you are legally married.

IN MISSOURI ...

... in the state of Missouri a law was passed stating that it was not illegal to speed.

IN MONTANA ...

... in the township of Whitehall it is illegal to operate a vehicle with ice picks attached to the wheels.

... it is illegal to have a sheep in the cab of your truck without a chaperone.

IN NEVADA ...

... it is illegal to drive a camel on the highway.

IN NEW JERSEY ...

... all motorists must sound their horns before passing another car, bicyclist, skater or skateboarder.

… drivers who have been convicted of being DUI cannot apply for a personalised licence plate.

… on a highway you cannot park under a bridge.

… you cannot pump your own gas. All gas stations are full service and full service only.

… under no circumstances may an automobile pass by a horse-drawn carriage whilst on the streets of New Jersey.

… car showrooms are banned from opening on a Sunday.

… courting couples in Liberty Corner must refrain from sexual intercourse in parked cars as they can face jail terms, especially if the car horn is inadvertently sounded during the act.

IN NEW MEXICO …

… during lunch breaks in Carlsbad no couple should engage in a sexual act whilst parked in their vehicle, unless the car is equipped with a curtain.

… it is illegal for women to pump gas. Instead, men must willingly volunteer to pump for single ladies. The same rule applies to flat tyres.

IN NEW ORLEANS …

… the law says that it is illegal for a woman to drive a car unless her husband is waving a flag in front of it.

IN NEW YORK …

… jaywalking is legal, as long as it's not diagonal. That is, you can cross a street at right angles to the sidewalk, but you can't cross it diagonally.

… members of nine New York Indian tribes are exempt from the city's 8% parking tax.

… it is a crime to accept a ride in a stolen vehicle, whether you know the vehicle is stolen or not.

… even silly parking meter regulations exist in some law offices and in downtown City Hall areas it seems there are only quarters-only parking meters. Apparently City Hall considers nickels and dimes passé.

… no blind person may drive or attempt to drive an automobile.

IN NORTH CAROLINA ...

... in the days when cars were a rare sight any motorist entering Forest City had to stop and call City Hall. The reason was to give people sufficient time to go out and hold their horses until the motorist had passed through.

... legislation exists in the township of Dunn stating that it is illegal to drive an automobile through a city cemetery for pleasure.

... in North Carolina it is a crime to operate or possess a device in a car that produces unusual amounts of smoke, gas or any other substance not necessary for the car's operation or maintenance. It is a felony not just to use such a device but to have one in the car whether it's attached or just inside the car.

IN OHIO ...

... cars are not allowed to scare horses in Centerville.

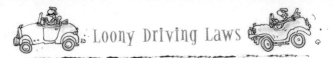

... a 'restricted' driver's license may be issued to a person who is 14 or 15 years of age upon proof of hardship to the Registrar of Motor Vehicles.

... whenever passing another car the car horn must be sounded.

... a police officer can write a ticket for leaving ignition keys in a car. You'll get them back so long as you can prove you're the owner.

... ' ... *no person while operating a motor vehicle shall fail to slow down and stop the vehicle when signalled to do so upon meeting or overtaking a horse drawn vehicle or person on horseback and to remain stationary until such vehicle or person has passed, provided such signal to stop is given in good faith under circumstances of necessity, and only as often and for such length of time as is required of such vehicle or person to pass, whether it is approaching from the front of rear.*'

... Power Wheels® cars may not be driven down the street in Canton

... it is illegal to run out of petrol in Youngstown.

... it is illegal for cab drivers in Youngstown to carry passengers on the roof of their vehicle.

IN OKLAHOMA ...

... no-one is allowed to molest an automobile in the township of Clinton.

... according to state law cars must be tethered outside public buildings.

IN OREGON ...

... between the hours of 9pm in the evening and 5am the following morning no vehicle may pass along or across a traffic congestion thoroughfare more than twice in the city of Portland.

... ' ... it is legal to own a car without a windshield, but illegal to own one without windshield wipers.'

... trucks may not be parked on the street in Portland.

... riders of sleds may not attach themselves to passing cars in Portland.

... it is illegal to carry a child on an extended part of a motor vehicle such as the hood, fender, running board or other external part of any motor vehicle that is upon a highway.

Loony Driving Laws

IN PENNSYLVANIA ...

... any motorist who sees a team of horses coming towards him must pull well off the road, cover his car with a blanket or canvas that blends in with the countryside, and let the horses pass. If the horses appear skittish the motorist must take his car apart piece by piece and hide it under the nearest bushes.

... it costs $50 a year to park in the centre of Carlisle but each evening the cars must be moved for street cleaning even if they are snowed or iced in.

... it is illegal to tie a horse to a parking meter in the township of Tarentum.

... any motorist driving along a country road at night must stop every mile and send up a rocket signal, wait 10 minutes for the road to be cleared of livestock and only then continue.

IN RHODE ISLAND ...

... it is illegal to coast downhill in your car with your transmission in neutral or with the clutch disengaged.

... it is illegal to drive down any street in Scituate with beer in your car, even if it is unopened.

... whenever a motorist is overtaking another motorist on the left they must make a loud noise.

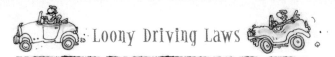
IN SOUTH CAROLINA ...

... performing a U-turn within 1,000 feet of an intersection is illegal.

... whenever motorists are approaching a four-way or blind intersection you must stop 100ft from the intersection and discharge a firearm into the air to warn other horse traffic.

... it is illegal to drive a motorised vehicle on King Street in Charleston.

IN TENNESSEE

... it is illegal for a woman to drive a car in Memphis unless there is a man either running or walking in front of it waving a red flag to warn approaching motorists and pedestrians.

... you cannot shoot any game other than whales from a moving automobile.

... state law bans any motorist from driving whilst they are asleep.

... no more than five inoperable vehicles are allowed on any single piece of property in Fayette County.

IN TEXAS ...

... it is forbidden in Jacques Village County to keep more than four inoperable vehicles in front of your house.

... in the township of Silvertone it is illegal to drive within three miles of the city limits.

... it is illegal in Lubbock County to drive within an arm's length of alcohol.

... it is illegal to have a camel run loose in the street in Galveston.

... it is illegal to place a 'for sale' sign on a car if it is visible from the street in Richardson.

... it is illegal to ride a horse at night in Texarkana without tail lights.

… it is illegal to drive down Broadway before noon on a Sunday in Galveston.

… car horns cannot be sounded in San Antonio.

IN UTAH …

… birds have the right of way on the highways.

… motorists who alter their license plate stickers on their vehicles in some cities could incur a $15,000 fine.

IN VIRGINIA …

… when overtaking other automobiles citizens must sound their horns.

… driving barefoot is banned.

… driving by the same place within 30 minutes on Atlantic Avenue, Virginia Beach is prohibited.

… in Prince William County it is illegal to park a car on railroad tracks.

IN WASHINGTON …

… a motorist with criminal intentions has to stop at the city limits and telephone the chief of police as they are entering the town.

… there is a $200 fine for drivers whose automobiles are not equipped with an ashtray.

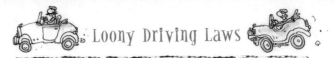

... you are allowed to transport an aquarium on public transport buses so long as the fish remain still.

... in the city of Vancouver all motor vehicles are required to carry anchors as an emergency brake.

IN WISCONSIN ...

... any owner whose vehicle should drip oil on to the pavements in the township of Green Bay will be fined $1 for each drip.

... in the city of Hudson no person may sit on another's parked vehicle without the expressed consent of the owner whether the vehicle is parked on a public street, alley, parking lot driveway or private premises.

… in the city of Sun Prairie riding a bicycle without your hands on the handlebar is illegal. According to the legislation ordained: *'No bicycle shall be allowed to proceed in any street in the city by inertia or momentum with the feet of the rider removed from the bicycle pedals. No rider of a bicycle shall remove both hands from the handlebars or practice any trick or fancy riding in any street in the city nor shall any bicycle rider carry or ride any other person so that two persons are on the bicycle at one time unless a seat is provided for the second person.'*